Y0-BED-051

Lefty Kreh's
Longer Fly Casting

New and Revised

Also by Lefty Kreh

Longer Fly Casting
Fly Fishing in Salt Water
Practical Fishing Knots
(with Mark Sosin)
Fly Casting with Lefty Kreh
Salt Water Fly Patterns

Lefty Kreh's Longer Fly Casting

New and Revised

The Compact, Practical Handbook That Will Add Ten Feet—Or More—To Your Cast

Lefty Kreh

THE LYONS PRESS

Guilford, Connecticut
An imprint of The Globe Pequot Press

To buy books in quantity for corporate use
or incentives, call **(800) 962–0973**
or e-mail **premiums@GlobePequot.com**.

Copyright © 1991, 2003, 2007 by Bernard "Lefty" Kreh
Illustrations © 1991, 2003, 2007 by Rod Walinchus

ALL RIGHTS RESERVED. No part of this book may be reproduced or transmitted in any form by any means, electronic or mechanical, including photocopying and recording, or by any information storage and retrieval system, except as may be expressly permitted in writing from the publisher. Requests for permission should be addressed to The Lyons Press, Attn: Rights and Permission Department, P.O. Box 480, Guilford, CT 06437.

The Lyons Press is an imprint of the Globe Pequot Press.

Printed in the United States of America

1 2 3 4 5 6 7 8 9 10

ISBN 13: 978-1-59921-087-2

The Library of Congress has previously cataloged an earlier
(paperback) edition as follows:
Kreh, Lefty.
Longer fly casting / Lefty Kreh; illustrated by Rod
Walinchus.
p.   cm.
Includes index.
ISBN 1-55821-127-6: $12.95
1. Fly casting. I. Title.
SH454.2.K72 1991
779.1'2—dc20 91-30223
CIP

CONTENTS

I never met a fly fisherman who did not want to be able to cast ten feet—or more—farther. The trout or tarpon or permit or bass always seem at least that distance beyond our best cast, and there is simply no adequate solution other than being able to make a longer cast.

Sometimes you may have plenty of room to engineer such longer casts—if you know how; but often, "longer" means ten feet added to a forty-foot roll cast or to some special cast determined by sharply restricted surroundings.

Of course we sometimes need more than ten feet to do the business at hand—and perhaps in the end what we really want are *principles* by which we can continue to lengthen our casts over a period of many years, through thoughtful practice.

For one of the great pleasures a lot of us take in all aspects of fly fishing is that we never learn it all, and always want to learn a little more.

This little handbook, graced with Rod Walinchus's clear drawings, will help you to refine your fly casting—to cast with more accuracy and authority but primarily for greater distance. It is a short, narrowly focused book, but an important one, we think—one that establishes principles to live with along with specific techniques. We hope you'll find Lefty an ebullient, innovative, and skillful teacher.

Nick Lyons

1 | Getting More Distance Out of Your Casts

For several hundred years, one method of fly casting has dominated the sport—that of duplicating the sweep of the hands on a clock face with the casting motions. This method also involves moving the rod through a relatively short arc. Let's look at how this method—so universal today—was developed.

Several centuries ago in Europe, anglers began using artificial flies, rather than live bait, to catch trout. Their tackle was crude. A long, often sixteen-foot, wooden rod, to which was attached several feet of braided horsehair and a short gut leader, allowed them to cast their flies across narrow streams. They determined that, with a long rod, if they started at about belt level with the rod tip (nine on the clock face) and swept up swiftly, stopping at about the twelve or one o'clock position, they could make an effective cast for the conditions they encountered. Until the middle of this century, casting instructors often had students hold a book under the elbow of the casting arm—in order not to drop the book, the caster had to limit the arc of his swing to within the nine-to-one area.

The book technique is no longer used, of course, but we are still teaching a method that was developed several centuries ago for conditions few modern anglers face. Tackle has changed dramatically. We no longer cast just on narrow meadow streams. Instead, we throw flies across wide steelhead and salmon rivers. We thrust a bonefish fly or bass bug into a stiff breeze. Those seeking billfish with a fly rod frequently are casting flies that are longer than some of the trout caught by those Europeans who developed the nine-to-one-o'clock method. Yet, and perhaps because fly fishing is so bound by tradition, we have not brought any real changes to that basic casting technique developed so long ago.

The method I have been advocating and teaching for many years is totally different from the conventional, centuries-old way. But let me first emphasize that the nine-to-one-o'clock method will allow a good caster to obtain long distances, and even throw large flies. But it requires a great deal more energy and effort than the method I suggest. Not only will you get more distance and easier casting with my method, but older folks, women, and people not possessing great strength can cast for considerable distances and long periods of time without tiring when using it. Both methods work. But mine will do the job easier, and will allow you to throw farther with less effort—and you will become a more accomplished caster faster than you would if you learned the older style.

With the modern method I urge you to try, you need to learn only four basic principles to make any practical cast. Once you understand these four principles, you can also evaluate your casting. Being able to critique your own casting is extremely valuable when you try to improve.

LEFTY'S METHOD OF CASTING

I believe that when using the conventional, less-efficient, style of casting, the double haul acts as a crutch. Once you master the method I suggest and then learn the double haul, longer casts will come much easier. My method does not refer at all to the clock face, and it asks you to discard much of what you have been taught about the traditional way to cast. Those who have never been exposed to conventional fly casting pick up my method quickly and do well. Those who have been using the conventional style of casting will find that they must forget many of the precepts of that style. Let's begin by examining my four principles of casting.

Regardless of the individual's casting style all casters are governed by the following four principles.

1. **You must first move the fly line end before you can make a back or forward cast.** This causes the rod to bend or load, storing energy. It is also good fishing technique to lift all line from the surface before making a backcast.

2. **Once the line is moving, the only way to load the rod is to move the casting hand at**

an ever-increasing speed and then bring it to a sudden stop. The sudden stop if often called a power stroke. Applying power spoils the cast. It should be called a speed up and stop stroke. The faster you accelerate the rod hand and then the faster you speed up and stop the rod tip, the faster the line will travel. The size of the loop is solely determined by the distance and direction the rod tip moves in the final moment of the cast during the speed up and stop.

3. **The line will go in the direction the rod tip speeds up and stops.** If on the backcast, the rod tip stops at any angle going up (or rising) the line will go straight. If the rod tip stops going down and back, then sag is produced in the line that must be removed before a forward cast can be made. With almost all forward casts, the rod tip should stop in a direction either parallel to or slightly climbing above the surface.

4. **The longer the distance the rod travels on the back and forward casting strokes the less effort is required to make the cast.** The shorter the rod moves through a casting stroke, the harder you must work to put the same load in the rod. When you need to cast farther, throw heavier flies, defeat the wind, or to make a number of special casts (even when trout fishing) the rod must travel farther back and forward. *Being able to take the rod well behind you on the backcast will allow you to make many different casts and produce more fish for you.*

Every fly caster has different physical make-up and there is no one exact way to cast if we want to accommodate all fishing conditions. A tall person will cast differently than one who is shorter and not as strong. When fishing you may have to make a side backcast and a vertical forward cast to deliver a fly to the fish. Instead of learning a specific method of casting I suggest learning the four principles of casting. This allows you to adapt your casting style to your physical makeup—and adjust the cast to current fishing conditions.

A principle is something we can't argue with. Two examples are water will run downhill and gravity affects all objects. A rule is man-made and can be changed. The four principles apply to everyone who casts. But the following three Aids to Casting can be violated since there are rules—but in doing so I believe you lose efficiency in your casting.

AIDS TO BETTER FLY CASTING

1. If you are right-handed, the right foot should be positioned to the rear and the left foot slightly forward. Left-handers should do the reverse. This allows the body and the arm to move easily back and forth.

2. Before you begin the backcast, the **thumb should be positioned behind the rod handle from the target.** The hand should not be twisted throughout the backcast. This accomplishes two things: (1) energy in the cast is better-transmitted back and forward and (2) accuracy improves.

3. **The elbow should not be elevated on the cast.** Imagine walking up to a shelf that is as

high as your elbow. Place your elbow on the shelf. Think that during the entire cast the elbow should remain in contact with the shelf regardless of how far back the elbow moves. The angle of the backcast is determined by the angle that the rod hand stops. But the elbow should not be elevated (or lifted from the shelf).

PICTURING THE PRINCIPLES
Lefty's Method—A Side View

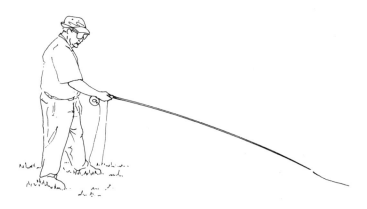

STEP 1 For a short cast the thumb should be behind the handle from the target and the wrist should not twist on the cast. If right-handed the right foot is slightly back. For a left-hander the left foot is positioned to the rear. Begin with the rod lowered close to the water. The rod hand will be brought a short distance vertically or angled to the side. Use very little wrist motion and cast mainly with the forearm. The more the wrist is flexed on the cast the more likely the loop will be too large. To eliminate a sag in the backcast line always stop the rod tip while it is rising in the direction you want the fly to go.

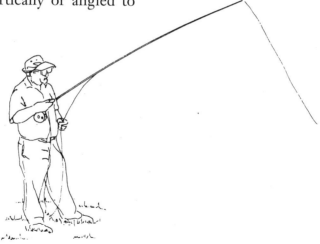

STEP 2 Lift the line from the water and accelerate back, speeding up and stopping the rod tip in the direction you want the line and fly to travel. The longer the cast, the longer the rod accelerates on the backcast. By moving the elbow along the imaginary shelf (not elevating it) and stopping the rod with a short speed up and stop at the end of the cast, the line will be without sag and there is a tight loop in the direction you want the fly to travel. The most effective backcast is one that is directed opposite the forward cast target.

STEP 3 A difference between this method and the conventional style is that you do not "drift" the rod after the rod is stopped on the backcast. It is the sudden stop that determines loop size and how fast the line travels to the target.

An angler who practices thousands of casts can learn to throw a good backcast by drifting. But a much quicker way to master throwing a fast-traveling tight loop backcast is simply to accelerate the rod as far back as desired and then come to an abrupt stop. For short casts the accelerated period is brief. For longer casts the acceleration is longer. At the end of the acceleration if the rod comes to a quick stop all of the energy of the cast is directed away from or toward the target.

STEP 4 For a longer cast the thumb should be behind the rod from the target. To obtain greater

body movement it helps to position the foot farther to the rear. If you bring the rod up vertically, you cannot take it further back without twisting the wrist (a flaw which will cause the line

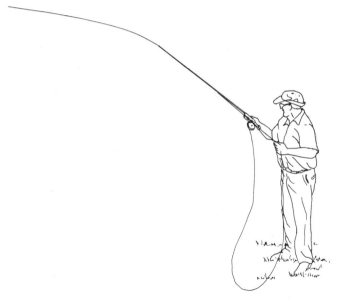

loop to roll outward and waste energy) or until you master drifting the rod.

Remember, to make an efficient, tight loop backcast without sag the rod hand must travel directly away from the target and the rod tip and hand must stop "upward" in the direction you want the backcast to go. This is accomplished easily if the forearm is rotated forty-five or more degrees away from the body. This permits the rod hand with the thumb behind the rod handle from the target and the elbow to move as far back as you want on the shelf, stopping the rod tip in the direction you want the line to travel on the backcast.

STEP 5 To begin the forward cast, start the rod hand forward before the line unrolls. If you wait until it straightens and then begin the cast, the line begins to fall creating sag that must be removed before a forward cast begins. The line loop should resemble a candy cane as you start forward.

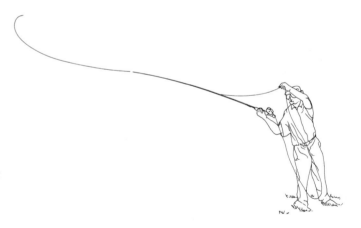

STEP 6 Continue to accelerate the forearm forward—using little or no flexing of the wrist to ensure a tighter loop. You should have kept the elbow on the imaginary shelf during the backcast. Continue to keep the elbow on that shelf during the forward cast. This directs all the energy toward the target. Elevate the elbow and you dissipate some of the energy away from the target and enlarge your loop.

STEPS 7 AND 8 The faster you accelerate the rod hand the more speed develops in the line and the deeper you bend the rod to store energy for the final moment in the cast. The fly will travel in the direction the rod tip speeds up stops and the rod straightens. It is critical to come to a quick stop and not lower the rod immediately. If you do you delete some of the energy away from

the target and pull open your loop. As the rod straightens it should remain there until the loop unrolls far enough away from the rod before you lower it. This can be accomplished easily by stopping the rod and mentally counting to three before lowering it.

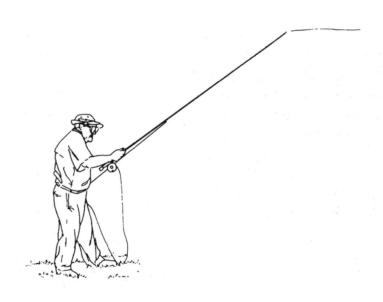

Lefty's Method—A Front View

In my method, the angle at which the rod travels is slightly different from the conventional style. On short casts, the thumb is on top of the rod handle, and the rod comes almost straight back. But on longer casts, the backcast is more of a sidearm cast only because the forearm can be moved in a straight line to well behind the body when doing this. Study the head-on as well as the side views in the drawings to see what I mean.

STEP 1 The forearm is rotated outward from the body about forty-five degrees, and the rod tip is pointing at the target and held very low. See how the reel is tilted at an angle. It will remain at that angle throughout the backcast.

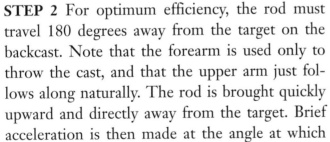

STEP 2 For optimum efficiency, the rod must travel 180 degrees away from the target on the backcast. Note that the forearm is used only to throw the cast, and that the upper arm just follows along naturally. The rod is brought quickly upward and directly away from the target. Brief acceleration is then made at the angle at which you want the line to travel. Note that the rod is still angled off to the side.

STEP 3 As soon as the backcast is made, the rod hand is brought around and in toward the body—*it travels in an oval*—and then moves straight toward the target.

STEP 4 The forward cast is made. What is important to understand from this front view is that the rod will travel in a side cast until the end of the backcast. Then it is brought around and straight forward. Viewed from overhead, the rod travels in a definite oval during the cast.

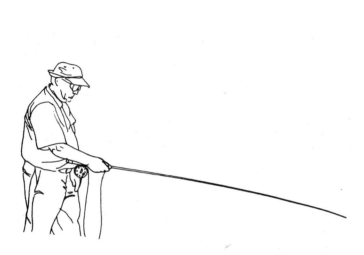

*The Conventional Cast and How the Hand
Travels during It*

STEP 1 The conventional method of casting requires that the thumb be held on top of the rod, as shown.

STEP 2 If the thumb remains on top of the rod handle on the backcast the hand can travel only this far before the body blocks further movement. This limits the distance you can move the rod back in a straight line.

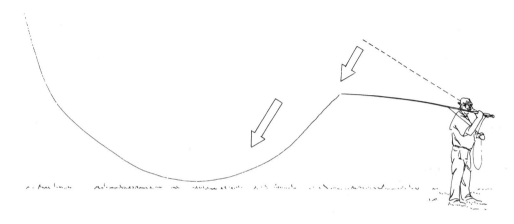

*The Effects of Bending and Not
Bending the Wrist*

VIEW 1 The conventional method asks you to bend your wrist to create a power stroke that throws the line at the target. My method advocates no "power" application, only a quick acceleration at the end of the cast. This drawing demonstrates how bending the wrist at the end of the cast develops wide loops and unwanted slack in the line.

Principle Number 3 says that the line is going to go in the direction that the rod tip is pointed when it stops. If the wrist is bent at the end of the backcast, as shown in the drawing, the line is going to travel down and back. That means that most of our forward rod motion will contribute nothing toward throwing the fly toward its target because of the pull of that slack. You cannot make a forward cast until you remove that deep sag in the line behind you.

VIEWS 2 AND 3 If the forearm and hand are stopped, with the wrist locked, after accelerating in a straight back-and-upward direction, the line will travel straight behind. There is no slack, so any forward movement of the rod will instantly begin moving all of the line and fly toward the target.

Loop size is determined by the distance the rod tip moves when accelerated at the end of the backcast. If the wrist bends, the tip travels over a much longer arc and the loop size increases.

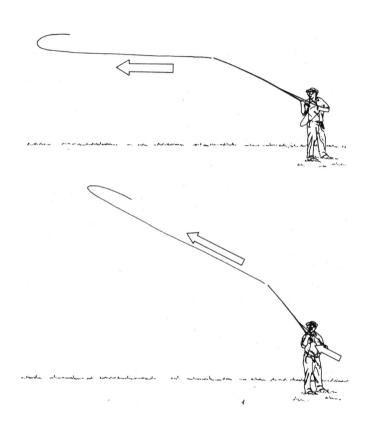

2

The Double Haul

To understand the double haul, the single most useful technique in casting is to understand that a fly line is not cast. Instead it is **unrolled**. When the rod tip is accelerated and stopped the line begins to unroll away from or back to the target. When the line unrolls completely or straightens the cast will fall. The length and speed of the double haul is determined by the job at hand.

When dry fly fishing you may make a single haul of a few inches but when throwing a big, wind-resistant fly on the ocean the haul may be very long.

To throw heavier or wind-resistant flies or a longer distance we need to deliver the fly and line to the target **before it unrolls**. This is accomplished by making the line travel faster so it arrives at the target before it unrolls. That is what double hauling accomplishes. I believe that almost all double haulers—even experienced fly fishermen who throw long lines—use only one component of a double haul. Should they add other components they will cast farther and easier.

An efficient double haul should mirror a rod stroke. A basic rod stroke with all types of tackle is comprised of an accelerated stroke and then the rod is brought to sudden stop. The faster the rod is accelerated the faster the lure, bait, or fly line travels and the deeper the rod bends, storing extra energy that contributes to the cast. The faster the rod tip stops the greater the amount of energy is directed away from or back to the target.

With this in mind let's examine how most people make a double haul—even experienced casters throwing long lines. As the rod hand accelerates on the cast the other hand pulls on the line. By pulling on the line two things are accomplished that complement the cast. The line travels faster and the rod bends deeper. The faster the hand pulls on the line the faster the line travels and the deeper the bend in the rod. What most fly casters do at the end of the cast is to suddenly stop the rod hand but they continue pulling with the line hand. It is the stop that delivers the line. If the line hand continues to pull after the rod hand stops some of the cast's energy is directed away from the target and usually the loop is enlarged. To improve the double haul the rod and the hand pulling the line should stop at the same time, maximizing all of the energy toward the target.

Remember that the faster the line travels forward and the deeper the bend the farther the line will travel on the cast. What most casters do when they want to throw an extra long cast is to overpower the rod and hand, which destroys their loop and often creates shock waves and a poor cast.

The line hand during double hauling should be considered a gearshift. Try a simple experiment to help your double haul. Make three false casts while observing the forward casts. Haul slower than normal during the first cast. On the second cast haul your normal speed and during the third cast haul much faster, trying not to add any extra effort to the rod hand. You will note that with a slow haul the line travels slowly, increase the haul faster and the line picks up speed and when you haul even faster the haul really improves the speed of the cast. The lesson here is that when you need more effort from the cast be sure to make a controlled cast with the rod hand but simply haul on the line faster.

STEP 1 Once learned, the single or double haul is used perhaps with 75 percent or more of fishing casts. The length of the double haul is determined by how difficult or how far you want to cast. A 20-foot cast to bluegills with a small popping bug requires a short single or double haul. But if you are throwing a long cast across a steelhead river or trying to get a big wind-resistant bass bug to a distant target a long, faster double haul may be needed.

STEP 2 A common problem with people who double haul is to make a long pull with the line hand and when the rod hand stops the line hand is several feet away from the rod butt. As the rod hand begins the forward cast, slack develops between the two hands. This slack must be removed with rod motion before the fly line begins moving forward. Frequently, this results in the line tangling around the reel or rod butt.

To eliminate both problems and make a more efficient double haul, the moment the rod hand stops the hauling should cease and the line hand should be brought to just in front of the rod butt. This eliminates that troublesome slack and makes it possible to haul longer on the forward cast.

3 | Some Basic Tips for Longer Casts

There are a few things fly fishermen can do to help put more distance in casts.

CLEAN LINES

Clean lines cast and shoot better. Dirt, grit, and grease that accumulate on a line create resistance when the line is shot through the guides.

For that reason anyone who desires to get maximum distance out of his or her cast will keep a line super clean. There are several methods of cleaning lines.

Perhaps the best way to clean a fly line is to use warm water and **soap**—never detergent. Detergent can remove some of the lubricant from modern lines, which makes the cast better. If the bottle doesn't say soap—it's probably detergent. A piece of terry cloth or old towel is the ideal thing to scrub the line with. Once cleansed all soap must be removed. Using a clean piece of terry cloth, place the line in cool, clean water and scrub the line well.

Some anglers use commercial vinyl cleaners such as Armor All. But such cleaners often remove some of the lubricant in the line and most are water solvent. They feel slick soon after application and shoot well through the guides, but the material soon dissolves in the water while fishing.

It is best to use a commercial fly line cleaner. If the cleaner has a silicone base, it is important to buff the line well to remove excess silicone. If left on the line, the sticky substance may pick up grit and dirt.

New lines cast well because there are clean. Floating lines begin to sink when they accumulate grit, grease, and dirt. Be careful not to drop the line on dirty surfaces. One of the great advantages of a stripping basket is the line tends to remain much cleaner when fishing.

FALSE-CASTING MORE LINE

When you want to throw a longer line, one of the most important things to do is to hold more line aloft during the false cast. For example, if you want to make a ninety-foot cast, if you can false-cast sixty feet of line, you are only thirty feet short of the goal, which means you need only shoot thirty feet of the line. Any time you want to make a longer cast, try keeping a longer length of line outside the guides.

HEAVIER LINES

When casting into a wind, many people will switch to a one-size-heavier line. For example, if they are using an 8-weight line, they will substitute a 9-weight line. But the heavier line will overload the rod tip and cause it to flex or bend deeper than normal on the cast. This will create larger line loops, which travel less distance. What should be done is to substitute one size *lighter* and *false-cast more line than normal*. The added weight of the extra amount of line being false-cast will properly load the rod without creating deeper than normal flexes or bends in the tip—that results in tight loops. And the thinner line will penetrate the wind better.

STRIPPING-GUIDE SIZE

Another important factor in making long casts is the size of the stripping or butt guide on the fly rod. This is the lower or largest guide, nearest the handle. I once worked with a large company on the design of fly rods. I had them build me a fly-casting machine that would make a cast while we recorded the results on videotape. We learned many interesting things. One of them was that a fly line that is released from the hand to be shot toward the target does not flow in a relatively straight line. Instead, it sweeps up toward the guide in wildly wavering motions. It often strikes the butt guide and then folds over, then is drawn back, and finally slithers through. All of this is wasted energy that will detract from a cast. If you are already a person who can throw a pretty fast line, you may have experienced the line completely wrapping around the butt guide in some instances.

To alleviate this problem, it's important to install a large-diameter butt guide. For rods that throw a fly line weight 7 or larger, I urge you to have at least a sixteen-millimeter guide installed—twenty-millimeter is even better. All spinning rods have larger butt guides to gather in the wavering loops of monofilament; to a lesser degree, this is exactly what a fly rod should do.

Many rod builders know that larger guides help improve shooting line on the cast. But cosmetics plays a part in selling tackle, and few people will purchase a rod with an oversized guide. Fortunately, you can install your own or find a rod builder who can replace the too-small guide with a bigger one.

VIEW 1 Look at the line as it wavers toward the butt guide. Note how the line tends to overlap the guide, then has to come back before it finally goes through. All of this motion steals energy from your cast.

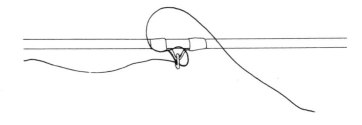

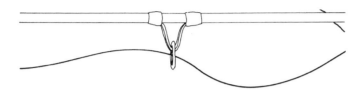

VIEW 2 Note how the larger guide funnels the line through better, increasing the distance of your cast.

CASTING FORM

There are two common mistakes in casting form that detract from obtaining distance and cause other problems. The first is footwork. Some fishermen make their casts with both feet standing even. This restricts body movement. Even worse is the tendency to place forward the foot on the same side as the arm handling the rod—that is, a right-hander with his right foot forward. This restricts body movement even more.

Your body on longer casts should move well back and then forward in a smooth, fluid motion. To obtain such free movement, it's vital that the foot on the side opposite the hand using the rod (left foot forward for a right-handed caster) should be placed well in front. Ignoring this principle of good form will affect your casting distance negatively.

The second common mistake is the tendency of many casters to hold the rod-arm elbow and upper arm too high during the cast. There are several reasons why this is bad. First, when the elbow and upper arm are elevated to or higher than the shoulder, all of the arm muscles tighten. This can be very tiring after repeated casting.

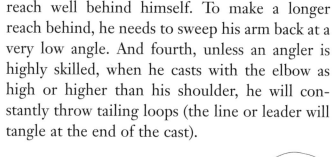

Second, raising the elbow higher than the shoulder restricts body movement and the ability to move smoothly. Third, with his elbow and upper arm higher than his shoulder, the angler cannot reach well behind himself. To make a longer reach behind, he needs to sweep his arm back at a very low angle. And fourth, unless an angler is highly skilled, when he casts with the elbow as high or higher than his shoulder, he will constantly throw tailing loops (the line or leader will tangle at the end of the cast).

4

More Distance in Basic
Casting Maneuvers

CONVENTIONAL ROLL CAST

The roll cast is necessary when a backcast can't be made because of some obstruction. Unfortunately, most people make poor roll casts that result in a pile of tangled line and leader falling to the water. Two common practices result in poor roll-cast performance: Keeping the rod in front on the roll cast, and directing the end of the cast downward, causing the line to be driven down and short of the target.

Four things must be done to accomplish an efficient roll cast. First, the rod must be brought back behind the body. Remember, the longer the rod travels through an arc, the more it helps the angler. Second, the rod needs something to pull against in order to load so that it can throw the line forward. To get that tension, the line must pause so water-surface tension can grip the line. Third, the cast is going to go in the direction the rod tip is pointing when it stops, so the end of the cast must be directed toward the target—not toward the surface in front of the angler. Fourth, the size of an unrolling line loop is determined by the distance the rod tip is moved quickly and then stopped at the end of the cast. Most people make a too-long speed-and-stop motion, resulting in a loop that is too open.

The Roll Cast

STEP 1 To begin the roll cast, *slide* the line back slowly on the water. Don't jerk or move it too quickly. Continue to move the rod back until it is well behind your body. Remember, *the longer the cast, the farther behind the body and rod should be*. On a very long cast the rod tip would be well behind the angler and nearly parallel to the water. Allow the line to come to a stop, or pause briefly. This lets the surface tension grab the line, so that when the rod comes forward, it has something to pull against. Stopping the line at this point is critical to good roll-casting.

STEP 2 *The forward roll cast should be made exactly like a conventional forward cast.* Sweep the rod forward, as in conventional casting. The faster and farther you want the cast to go, the faster and shorter the distance you must accelerate—speed up and stop—at the end of the cast.

STEP 3 *You must direct the energy or force of the cast at about eye level toward the target.* If you drive the rod downward, you will cause the cast to be directed toward the surface in front of you. As soon as the rod stops at eye level, you can lower it to the fishing position.

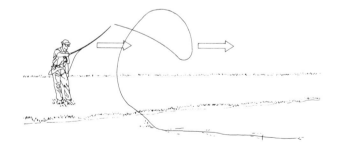

STEP 4 The two greatest faults of anglers who do not roll cast well is that they don't allow the line to pause when they are sliding it back, so that surface tension can grip the line, and they complete their forward casts with the rod tip driving toward the water in front of them. The cast must be directed *at* the target. To prove this point to yourself, make a normal cast, directing the fly and line toward the target at about eye level. Then, make another normal cast and end the forward motion by driving the tip downward in front of you. The first cast will fly toward the target. The second will cause the front of the line to crumple into a pile, as most people's roll casts do.

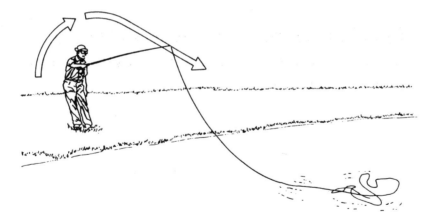

SINGLE WATER HAUL

Once the roll cast is mastered, getting more distance with a sinking line or a sinking shooting head is easy. When using a sinking line, most anglers bring in enough line so that they can make an aerial roll cast. When the fly leaves the water, they make a backcast, then a forward cast. But the backcast is made by pulling against air, which is not the best way to load a rod. The following illustrations demonstrate the single water haul, which pulls line against water tension to load the rod more effectively.

STEP 1 To make a single water haul, make a conventional roll cast. *Be sure to direct the cast straight ahead, at eye level, as shown.*

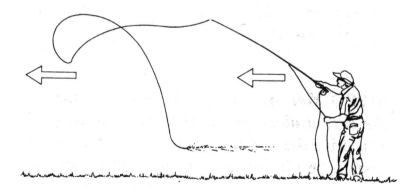

STEP 2 *The moment the rod stops its forward motion, drop the tip toward the surface.* (If you are using a sinking line, don't allow it to drop below the surface.) The moment the line unrolls and touches the water, you are ready to make the backcast. Draw the rod back, pulling on the line while the water's surface tension is gripping it. This loads the rod for the backcast.

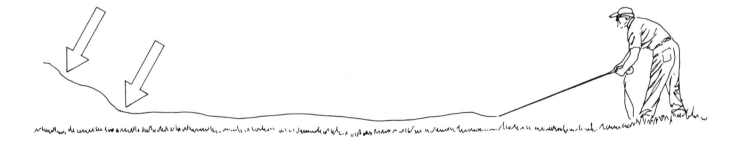

STEP 3 The moment you feel the rod is well loaded, make a conventional backcast. Because you have loaded the rod so well by pulling against the water, you'll get a faster backcast, which will result in a longer forward cast.

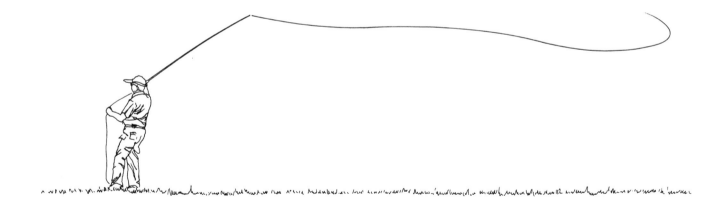

DOUBLE WATER HAUL

An advantage of the double water haul is that on the forward cast the line travels high above the angler's body. Fly casters who have thrown lead core shooting heads and other heavy weighted lines often do what is called "the lead core lurch": The angler makes the forward cast and then ducks low, hoping the line or fly doesn't strike him. The double water haul allows you to throw the fly and line high over your head.

STEP 1 Make a conventional roll cast and follow the procedure for making a single water haul.

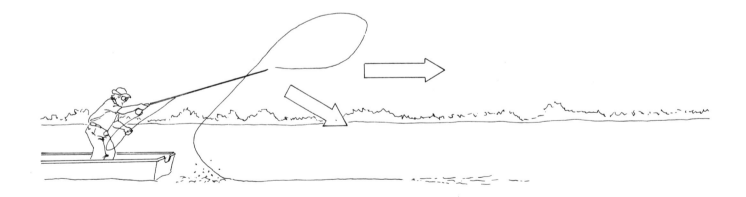

STEP 2 Allow the line to straighten, the same as for a single water haul.

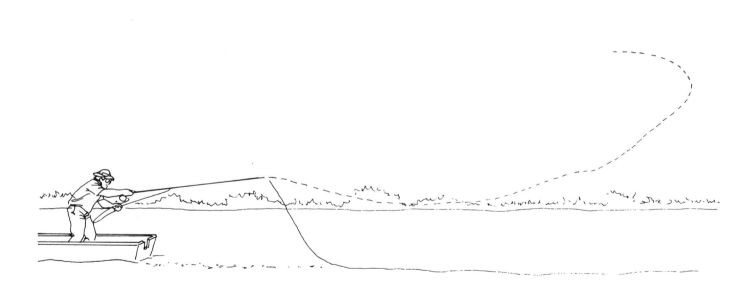

STEP 3 Instead of making a strong backcast, make a weak one—with just enough force to lay the line softly, straight behind you. Drop the rod tip low, as shown.

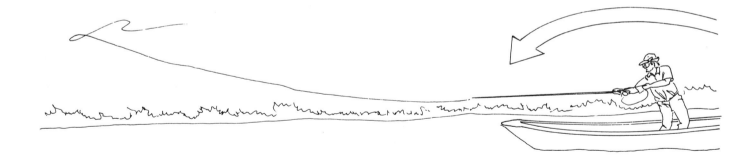

STEP 4 Watch the line as it unrolls on the back-cast. If you're using a sinking line, don't let it drop below the surface or you won't be able to pick it up. The key is to watch the end of the line: The moment it touches the water, start a long drawing-forward motion.

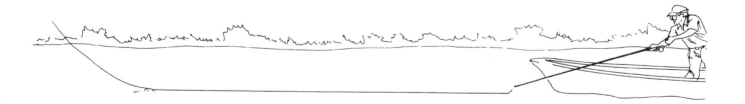

STEP 5 When you feel the rod is well loaded, make a conventional forward cast, aiming it high overhead, as illustrated. Because you have drawn the line against the water's surface tension, you will load the rod well, and thus increase your casting distance.

DISTANCE ROLL CAST

European anglers have been using spey casts and two-handed rods for many years to roll their lines back out for the next drift. Their technique is to place considerable line behind themselves before making the forward cast. With a conventional roll cast as practiced in the United States, very little of the line is placed back of the angler prior to the forward cast. Instead, the line is brought around beyond the angler, then the angler turns and rolls the line forward. All of this wastes energy.

A number of years ago, West Coast steelheaders adapted the spey cast for use with their single-handed rods. With this technique, an angler can roll even a weight-forward line eighty or ninety feet.

STEP 1 Slide the line back on the surface as if you were going to make a conventional roll cast.

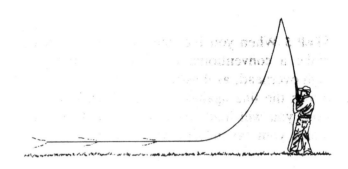

STEP 2 This step takes practice, but it's the key to the distance roll cast. When your rod hand is about a foot in front of your face and slightly lower than your chin, lift back and up smoothly in a curved arc (note the curved arrow in the illustration). This is the angle at which you should lift the rod to drop the line behind you.

Don't go straight back, or you'll throw a weak conventional backcast. Sweeping upward and backward will lift much of the line off the water in front of you and deposit it behind you.

STEP 3 *Make sure your rod extends well in back of you. As soon as the line falls to the water behind you,* make a long forward sweep to load the rod.

STEP 4 When you feel the rod is well loaded, accelerate a short distance and stop quickly. The drawing shows the perfect place to stop on the forward cast.

STEP 5 The line is pulled forward easily, and a long roll cast results.

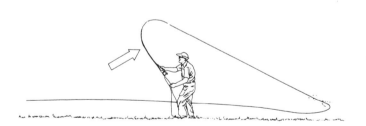

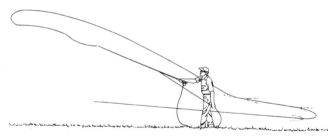

5 | More Distance with a Shooting Head

A shooting taper, which I will refer to as a shooting head, is a heavy length of fly line—usually thirty feet long—to which is attached a much thinner line. The thinner line is usually called a "shooting line." Shooting lines allow anglers to make longer casts. When released on the forward cast, the heavier head outside the rod tip drags the shooting line great distances. Distances of a hundred feet or more are common with rods size 7 or larger. All fly lines begin to fall to the water when they open and the loop unrolls. You can make shooting heads that will travel farther before opening—thus contributing to even greater distance on casts.

Use double-taper lines (they work better than forward tapers when modified as I will describe). If you are a good caster, cut thirty-five feet from one end of a double-taper line that is one size larger than the rod calls for. (For example, if you are using an 8-weight rod, use a number 9 double-taper line.) If you are not a good caster, you may want to try trimming only thirty-three or thirty-four feet. If you can handle a long line, try a forty-foot length. If you have any doubts, cut the line a little longer than I've recommended and cast it. If it seems to be unwieldy or difficult to handle, shorten it to the specifications mentioned. This is your modified shooting head.

You can attach a loop to the rear of the modified shooting head, but I have always felt that loops, no matter how small, are cumbersome and either rattle in or catch on the rod guides. However, they do offer the advantage of allowing you to change heads quickly. But if I'm using either commercial level shooting lines or braided leader material in long lengths, I prefer to attach them permanently to the rear of my shooting heads. To do this with a commercial level line, remove the finish from the end of it and the head. Sew them together with size A fly-typing thread, then overwrap the sewn area with the thread on a bobbin to make a super-smooth connection. Braided line can be slipped over the back of a modified head, then glued and wrapped, which also furnishes a very smooth connection.

There are a number of different kinds of shooting lines. Two are thin conventional fly lines. One matches a number 2 level line, and the other a number 3 level line. The thinner line sometimes tests less than fifteen pounds, so it's not recommended for tangling with powerful fish where the leader exceeds the test of the shooting line. The larger shooting line tests above twenty-five pounds and is preferred by many people, even though a few feet of distance are sacrificed because it is a little thicker and heavier. The advantage of using these thin fly lines for shooting lines is that they handle well and rarely tangle. The disadvantage is that they are heavier than other types of shooting line.

Another kind of shooting line is made from braided leader material. Ultrafine strands of monofilament are braided into a line similar to that of the braided butt section of some leaders. The advantage of this braided line as a shooting line is that it is very limp, shoots through the guides well, and rarely tangles. The disadvantage is that it has a rough surface, and many people find that it cuts their hands.

The first shooting heads had a shooting line of monofilament. The limp monofilament used in these lines is usually of twenty- to thirty-pound test. The lighter mono is used on lines weighted 5 through 7. For saltwater fishing, heavier thirty-pound is usually preferred. Monofilament shooting lines offer several advantages. Because they have a smooth, slick surface, they shoot through the guides better than any other type. They are also thinner and lighter than other shooting lines, which allows the shooting head to travel a greater distance. They have two disadvantages: They are sometimes difficult to hold on to when fighting a fish; and because the monofilament is so light, it tends to blow around during false-casting.

TRICKS TO HELP YOU GET MORE DISTANCE WITH A SHOOTING HEAD

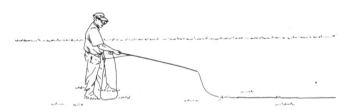

STEP 1 The amount of shooting line falling outside the rod tip is called "overhang." To obtain maximum distance, an angler should use as much overhang as possible. The correct amount of overhang is determined by an angler's casting ability and the rod outfit used. Thus, two separate anglers using the same outfit will use different lengths of overhang. And one angler with two different outfits may need four feet of overhang with one rod and five feet with the other. To determine if you have a correct amount of overhang, extend two to three feet of shooting line outside the rod tip. With the rod tip low to the water, begin a backcast.

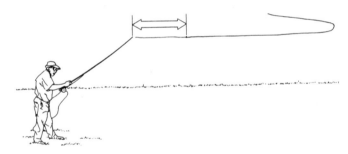

STEP 2 Make several false casts and watch your shooting head. As long as you do not have too much overhang, the line will unroll smoothly, as shown.

STEP 3 Gradually work out more overhang, because additional overhang will increase your distance potential. The moment you have too much overhang, you will see your shooting head begin to vibrate. This is because the thinner shooting line cannot support the heavy head.

STEP 4 Gradually retract the length of overhang until the vibrations disappear. The point at which the vibrating stops indicates the greatest length of overhang you can handle with that particular outfit. Now you are ready to make the final backcast.

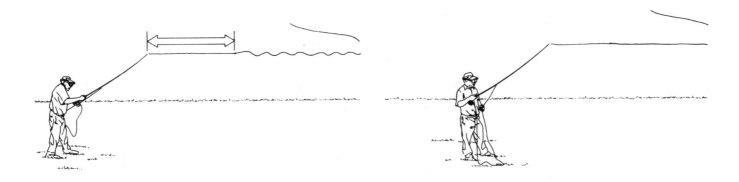

STEP 5 To obtain greater distance, add one more trick. As the *last* backcast is made, shoot as much line behind you as is equal to the length of your overhang. Then trap the line, and come forward hauling as you do so. By shooting this extra line on the backcast, you can add many feet to your final forward cast.

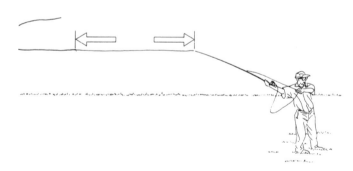

6 | Special Casting Problems

THE LONG-LINE PICKUP

A major problem for many casters is picking up a long line lying on the water's surface. Most anglers begin experiencing problems at about forty feet. When you understand *why* this is so difficult, and how to overcome the problem, lifting even eighty feet of line from the surface won't be too hard for you.

Surface tension grips a fly line that is floating on the water—it doesn't want to let the line go. That's why it is so important to stop the line as you take it back to make a roll cast. This stop allows surface tension to grasp the line so the rod has something to pull against to load itself. Surface tension is a plus factor with a roll cast, but with a conventional backcast it will inhibit your attempt to lift a long line from the surface. In making a long-line pickup, all fly line must be removed from the water before the backcast is begun.

It is also important that the pickup starts with the rod tip touching the water. The higher the tip is off the surface when you begin a backcast, the less amount of line you can lift. Follow the four steps shown here, and you'll be able to lift large amounts of line from the surface.

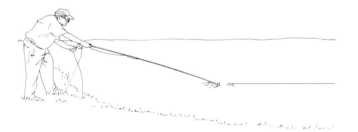

STEP 1 Lower the rod tip to the water, pointing it in the direction of the fly. Bend over and lean

forward: This allows you to lift a little more line than you could from an upright position. Use your line hand to remove all slack from the line.

STEP 2 As soon as all slack has been removed, reach forward and grasp the line as close as you can to the butt or stripping guide.

STEP 3 Raise the rod, *but try to keep your line hand in the position you started with—close to the butt guide.* When you think you have lifted as much line from the surface as you can, pull downward with the line hand, which will allow you to lift even more of the line. At this point, if you have made all the right moves, most of the fly line will lift from the surface, and only the leader and fly will remain there.

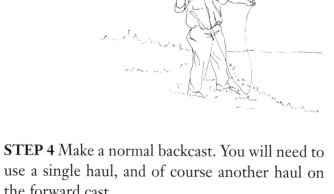

STEP 4 Make a normal backcast. You will need to use a single haul, and of course another haul on the forward cast.

CASTING WITH THE WIND AT YOUR BACK

Many fly casters curse the wind, but when the wind is at your back it can help you make a longer cast—if you use it to your advantage. If you can make a tight loop on the backcast, the wind at your back will help you cast longer than you normally could.

STEP 1 Make a low, tight-loop backcast to the side that tilts slightly downward but doesn't hit the water behind you.

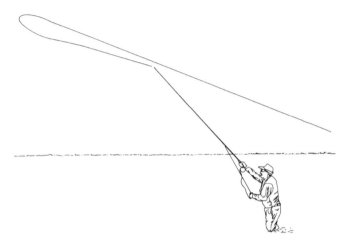

STEP 2 Make the forward cast at an upward angle, as shown. The line will be carried forward by the wind a great distance. The higher the angle the cast is directed, the more the wind will assist in carrying the line forward. In effect, you have turned the line into a kite for the wind to push. Once you master this cast, you will throw more line than your reel can hold.

CASTING INTO THE WIND

The major problem with casting into the wind is that once the line straightens, it tends to be blown until the leader falls in a tangled mess. The key is to throw the cast so that the fly is aimed directly at the

with a quick stop at the end of the cast—to throw the line into the teeth of the wind.

STEP 1 Make a relatively high cast at about the angle shown in the drawing. The longer you want the cast, the farther back your arm should be at the end of the backcast.

target. As soon as the line straightens, the fly falls to the surface and cannot be blown back. It helps to make the tightest loop you possibly can—which means making the shortest acceleration coupled

STEP 2 On the forward cast, direct the line so the fly is driven right at the target area. Your goal is to deliver the cast so the fly touches the surface when the leader unrolls. Then the wind will not be able to blow the line and fly backward.

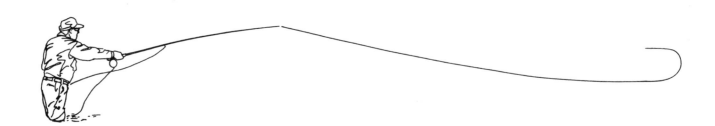

WIND BLOWING TOWARD THE ROD SIDE OF THE ANGLER

One of the most frustrating things that can happen when you are fly casting is wind blowing directly against your rod side. This makes it possible for the fly or line to hit you on both the back and forward casts. Some anglers will try to cast backhanded in this situation, but that's not very satisfactory because such a cast restricts natural arm motions and makes for inefficient casting. The best way to eliminate the problem is to learn to cast with either hand. When there is a wind on the right, simply switch the rod to your left hand. But because most fly fishermen aren't going to do that, here is a method of help you defeat the wind.

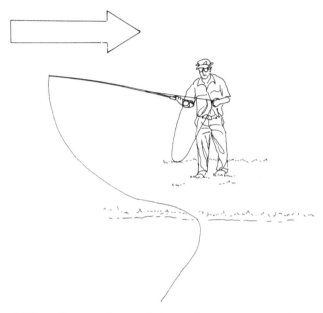

STEP 1 Lower the rod tip to the surface, and point it at the fly. Then begin a sidearm cast, as shown. This will carry the line well away from you, so it won't hit you on the backcast.

STEP 2 As soon as the backcast ends, sweep the rod in toward your body.

STEP 3 Make a conventional forward cast, with one difference. You know the wind is going to blow the line, so count on it! Don't tilt the rod slightly, as we usually do on a forward cast. Instead, during the very last stages of the cast *make sure the rod travels perfectly vertically.* The breeze will cause the line to blow downwind of you, and it will pass harmlessly by. Finish the cast as you would any normal forward cast.

THE CHANGE-OF-DIRECTION CAST

There are many fishing situations where you need to make a quick change of direction after the cast has been started. Perhaps a trout rises to one side or a bass crashes against some reeds to your left or right, and you need to get the fly there immediately. Or you have cast slightly upcurrent in a river and the fly has drifted downstream: You then want

to return the fly to the point where you started the first drift. Such casts are easy to make with a moderate amount of line—up to about forty feet.

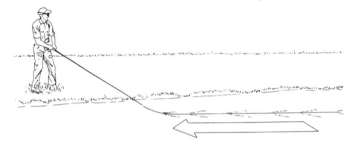

STEP 1 With the rod to your left, let's say a cast directly to the front is desired. Hold the rod inches above the water, and sweep the rod tip to

the side, drawing the line along the water. You want to keep as much line on the water as possible to aid in loading the rod on the backcast.

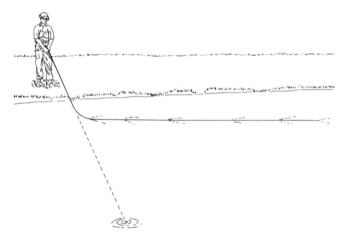

STEP 2 Continue to sweep the rod, keeping the tip low to the surface, until it is pointing at the target area.

STEP 3 As soon as the rod tip points at the target, make a backcast directly opposite the target. It is vital that you don't stop when the rod tip points at the target. If you stop, the line end will stop, and you'll have difficulty making the cast.

STEP 4 As soon as the backseat unrolls, make a conventional forward cast to the target.

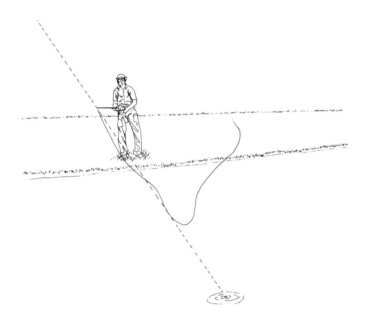

THE RIGHT-ANGLE CAST

A problem that comes up frequently for trout fishermen, and occasionally for other anglers, is that a cast is needed when there is a high obstruction directly behind them. This is where a right-angle cast helps. Such a cast can only be made well to about thirty-five feet, but casts within that distance can be made with less than five feet of clearance behind.

STEP 1 Stand parallel to the obstruction and make a normal backcast. Be sure to extend your rod hand well behind your body.

STEP 2 Bring your rod hand forward until it is even with your body. Remember, the line will go in the direction that the rod tip is pointing after it accelerates and stops. So at this point, move your casting hand ninety degrees to the side, so that it points at the target.

Step 3 Don't start accelerating your rod hand until the right-angle turn toward the target is made. Finish the acceleration and stop with the rod tip pointing in the direction you want the fly to go. You'll find the line sweeps forward alongside the obstruction behind you, then turns at a right angle and drops the fly where you want it.

WHEN THERE IS LITTLE BACKCAST ROOM

When you have only a little backcast room, twenty-five feet, for example, you can still make a cast to fifty or more feet in front of you. The key is not to make a standard backcast, which travels fast and straight behind. Instead, make a *circular* backcast—one that travels in a large oval.

STEP 1 Before making the actual cast, practice this little technique to help learn the cast quicker. Allow about twelve feet of line to extend beyond the rod tip. Begin rotating your rod hand in a circle. Keep continuous pressure on the line as your hand travels around the circle. This will force the rod to pull constantly on the line, and the line will follow the path in which the tip travels. If you do this properly, the line should travel as shown in the drawing. Once you master this trick, making a backcast when there is little room will be no problem.

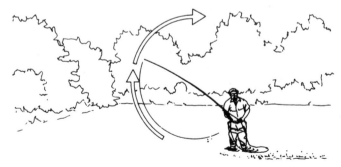

STEP 2 If you have an obstruction behind you about twenty-five feet, put out about thirty or thirty-five feet of line. Make a backcast by rotating the rod hand in a half circle, as shown. Be sure you apply constant rod pressure on the line around the half circle. Because the line will be traveling in a circle to the side, none of it will touch the obstruction.

STEPS 3 AND 4 When the rod reaches the point directly above your head, accelerate your rod hand quickly toward the target to make a tight loop. It pays to make a single haul at this point. If you make the cast correctly, you will have generated enough line speed so that you can shoot another fifteen to thirty feet of line to the target. With some practice, you'll be able to throw your fly a considerable distance with little room for your backcast.

THROWING AN EXTRA-HIGH BACKCAST, OR A BACKCAST INTO AN OPENING

There are times when a high bank, trees, or a wall is behind an angler. A high backcast is needed to get the line and fly above the obstruction. There are also occasions where there is an opening in the trees to the rear, and if the angler could backcast into the opening, he could make a longer forward cast.

What most anglers try to do in these situations is to make a conventional backcast above the obstruction or into the opening. This strategy usually ends in disaster because the line is going to travel in the direction the hand is aiming when it stops at the end of the cast. If you make a backcast in the normal manner and try to throw it higher, your hand points on the stop in the direction of the obstruction. And if you try to throw your normal backcast into a small opening in the trees, you most likely will throw a wider loop and end up with your fly caught in the trees.

Here is an improved method that allows you to throw longer backcasts and higher ones, too. It also allows a much more accurate cast into an opening.

STEP 1 How you start the cast is important. Touch the rod tip to the water, as shown. Invert your rod hand so that the rod is held upside down, with the reel pointing up and your thumb on the down side. With your thumb underneath like this, you can stop your hand on the acceleration at a much higher angle. And for casting into an opening, you'll essentially be making a forward cast behind you. Almost all anglers make a better, more controlled forward cast than they do a backcast—so this method improves their chances of throwing the fly into an opening behind them.

STEP 2 You should never make a backcast until you get the end of the line moving and all line off the water. Regardless of the amount of line on the surface when you start the cast, if you lift the rod tip smoothly and swiftly, by the time your rod hand has reached the position in the drawing, all line will be off the surface.

STEP 3 Accelerate the rod tip and stop when the tip points in the direction you want to go—either above the obstruction, or into an opening.

STEP 4 As soon as the stop is made, rotate your hand back to a normal position.

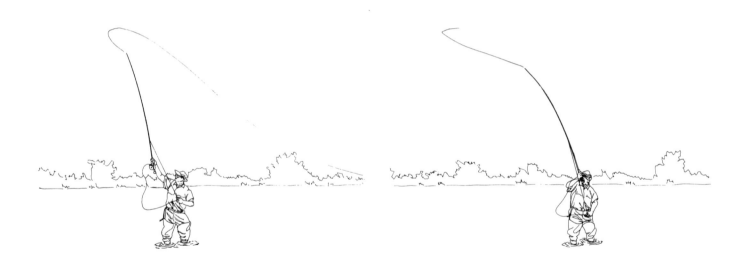

STEP 5 Bring the rod forward to get the end moving, as you would for a normal forward cast.

STEP 6 Finish as you would a normal forward cast.

CONTROLLING LINE ON THE SHOOT

A major mistake made by many, even experienced, fly fishermen when they throw a long line is to let go of it with the line hand. Three undesirable things can happen if the line is allowed to shoot uncontrolled through the guides.

One, because the line is flowing freely, it will often wrap around the rod guide or, worse, the handle or the reel. Two, if the line is released, its flight cannot be controlled. Three, when the line touches the surface, the angler has no control until it is recovered. Should a strike occur, or the fly need to be manipulated, the angler is unprepared.

VIEW 1 This is how many anglers release line on the shoot, allowing it to flow uncontrolled.

VIEW 2 By forming a ring with the thumb and first finger of the line hand and holding it around the shooting line below the first guide, the angler maintains control throughout the line's flight. At any time, the fly can be stopped and dropped on the target. The line doesn't have a chance to tangle with the rod; and when the fly settles to the water, instant control of it is ensured.

CONTROLLING A LONG LINE WHEN WADING

When you are fishing with a longer line and are forced to retrieve it while wading, you may have a problem handling the line stripped in during that retrieve. If you're standing in current, the line will be swept downstream and have to be yanked back before anything can be done with it. And when wading for bonefish, the line will trail along behind you, and will have to be recovered before it can be cast. There is a method that allows you to retrieve at least thirty feet of line and keep it under control. It takes a little practice to master, but once learned is a blessing.

VIEW 1 The cast has been made and the retrieve begins. When about ten feet of line have been recovered, slide the line back to the joint between the thumb and index finger on your line hand and trap it there. So the line doesn't slip, close the joint firmly.

VIEW 2 Continue to strip in line. When approximately ten more feet of line have been recovered, trap the line between the middle joint of your thumb and your index finger. By pressing your thumb against your first finger, you'll hold a line securely while you continue to strip more line. When another ten feet of line is taken in, trap it with the end of your thumb against your index finger.

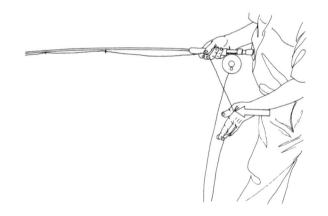

VIEW 3 You are now ready to make a backcast. If you've kept your thumb pressed against your index finger, all three coils of line will be under control during casting.

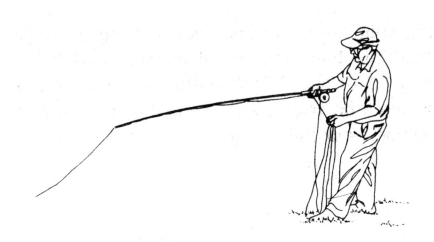

VIEW 4 Come forward after your backcast to make a forward cast. Until you become proficient with this method, it's a good idea to make the forward cast, shoot the topmost coil, make a backcast, and on a final forward cast shoot the other two coils. Once you have mastered the cast, you can end the stripping retrieve, make a backcast and shoot the first coil (using a double haul to help you), and shoot the other two coils as you come forward. In other words, in a single back and forward cast, you'll be able to shoot the line while keeping the length of retrieved line under control.

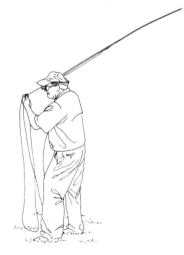

VIEWS 5 AND 6 Notice how the fingers are held
open to allow the line to flow off on the final for‐
ward cast.

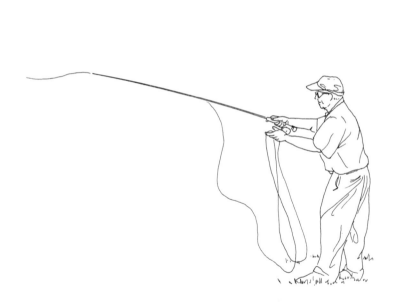

THE BASEBALL THROW

This versatile cast allows you to do several things. First, it will let you throw a dry fly into the teeth of the wind with authority. You'll be surprised how well you can turn over even an eleven- or twelve-foot leader in a stiff breeze. Second, there are many times when a long cast must be made, but the line and fly have to be kept close to the water. An example would be throwing well back under a pier or dock, or driving a fly under an overhanging bush at the water's edge. And third, there are situations in which an angler may want to throw a long line into a stiff wind while keeping line and fly close to the surface throughout their flight. The Baseball Throw is the cast for all these situations. I chose that name because you make this cast close to the way you throw a baseball. On a very short ball toss, the throwing hand doesn't go back very far. But when you want to make a long throw, you pull your hand well in back of your body—as you will in this cast.

STEP 1 Begin a backcast so that your arm is fully extended, but keep your elbow on the shelf. God rarely lets us make a perfect backcast, so we must remove any slack before we move the fly. An asset of this cast is that you can remove more slack than you would with a conventional backcast.

STEP 2 Here is where this cast differs from almost all other conventional casting motions. The rod is carried forward and remains parallel to the water surface until your hand is even with your shoulder. This is one of the very few casts where I recommend you bend your wrist during the cast—it is necessary in order to bring the rod forward while keeping it parallel to the water.

STEP 3 The angler is turning back toward the target while drawing his rod forward. When the angler is facing the target and the rod hand has come even with his shoulder, he should straighten his wrist and raise his elbow until it is just below the shoulder. Forearm and hand now travel parallel to the ground and straight forward. Unless you use this motion, you won't be able to make the cast properly.

STEP 4 The wrist is now straight and the thumb is on top of the rod handle. At this point, make an incredibly short and high-speed acceleration—*being sure that the tip travels exactly parallel to the surface toward the target area*. Then come to a quick stop. If the rod is accelerated at an up or down angle, the line will travel up or down. But if the tip accelerates parallel to the surface, and straight ahead, the line will travel at that angle. Remember this important principle: *The line is going to go in the direction the tip is accelerated and where it stops.*

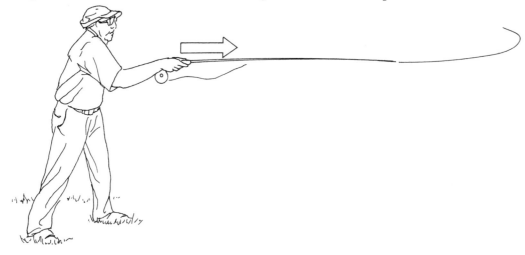

INDEX